YEAR 4

First Published in the UK in March 2018 by Focus Education (UK) Ltd

Focus Education (UK) Ltd
Talking Point Conference and Exhibition Centre
Huddersfield Road
Scouthead
Saddleworth
OL4 4AG

Focus Education (UK) Ltd Reg. No 4507968

ISBN 978-1-911416-19-7

Companies, institutions and other organisations wishing to make bulk purchases of books published by Focus Education should contact their local bookstore or Focus Education direct:

Customer Services, Focus Education, Talking Point Conference and Exhibit
Huddersfield Road, Scouthead, Saddleworth, OL4 4AG
Tel 01457 821818 Fax 01457 878205

www.focus-education.co.uk
customerservice@focus-education.co.uk
Printed in Great Britain by Focus Education UK Ltd, Scouthead

C000193502

Introduction

- The aim of this publication is to help teachers build on their current teaching repertoires and widen the range of activities that put greater emphasis on thinking and reasoning.

- Each of the sixteen ideas are supported by examples to help provide greater clarity. Clearly, the examples are just that, but should provide enough guidance for teachers to create the same method with the learning they are covering with their pupils.

- The aim is to help teachers 'teach less' and to increase the learning demands on pupils. The activities should put greater demand on pupils' thinking and reasoning skills.

- These methods require pupils to develop their curiosity and should help them to improve their own questioning. Therefore using these methods should help to create 'enquiry based classrooms'.

- In addition, many of the methods outlined will require learners to work as critical friends and evaluate each others' learning.

- The principles associated with 'metacognition' form a very important part of the process and the tasks take this into account.

- Only one mathematics example has been included because there are numerous examples of developing thinking and reasoning in mathematics already available.

- The publication starts with a reminder of what gets in the way.

Great Teaching?
What can get in the way?

Over-teaching

- **Teachers being the hardest working individual in a class**

- Too frequently, teachers with the best will in mind provide pupils with too much information that they could work out for themselves.
- Introductions can often be too lengthy.
- Sometimes it is the need to feel that, as a teacher, it is your job to inform the pupils.

- In too many cases, this results in pupils' learning being compromised.

What can get in the way?

Carpet

- **Pupils on carpet for too long, or too often.**

- In many of these cases it is the teachers' insecurities that come to the fore.
- It is almost a case of wanting to stretch their arms around the class so as to keep control of what is happening.
- The other issue that can happen is that additional adults in the room become passive and this important resource is not utilised appropriately.

What can get in the way?

Worksheet Overload

- **Keeping pupils occupied rather than developing their thinking.**

- An over-use of worksheets often occurs when the teacher tries to keep pupils busy rather than deepening their learning.
- In many cases it is an attempt to provide information that pupils then use as a comprehension exercise.
- One of the other issues is that the worksheets can be too 'samey'. In other words worksheets can often restrict the variety of activities provided for pupils.

What can get in the way?

It has to be in their books

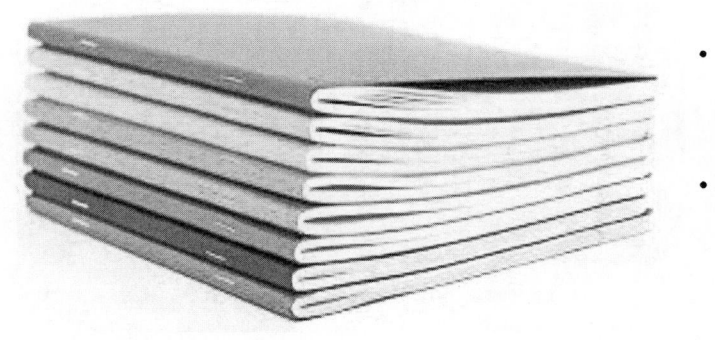

- **Learning hasn't taken place unless there is evidence in books!!!**

- In many respects this is understandable, especially with the focus on scrutiny that has happened during inspections.
- Many excellent 'thinking and reasoning' activities do not lend themselves to being recorded in exercise books (in traditional ways).
- We need to accept that sometimes photographs or a recording of a presentation, given by a group tell the story of the learning.
- The use of QR codes also provides another way of showing the outcomes

What can get in the way?

The answer is in my head

- **Questioning to match what's in teacher's head.**

- This occurs when the teachers falls into an over-long 'question and answer' routine.
- Too frequently the question asked by the teacher requires one answer and is therefore closed.
- Sometimes there can be a number of answers but the teachers moves around the class until someone matches the answer they have in their head.

What can get in the way?

Transfer of Knowledge

- **See teaching as transferring knowledge**

- In these instances there is little opportunity for developing pupils' thinking or reasoning.
- This is often a didactic method of teaching.
- It limits what can be taught or learnt and provides little opportunity for pupils to think for themselves.
- This form of teaching tends to occur when the teacher is insecure and does not pupils to move away from their script.

So what do we need?

- Enquiry-focused classrooms

- Pupils asking more questions

- Greater range of teaching methods

- Collaborative learning

- Links in the learning

- Curriculum Cohesion

What can we do?

Here are sixteen ideas to help widen teaching methodologies

- *The sixteen listed here are explained in the following pages*

1	Drawing on prior learning	9	Providing a starting point
2	Creating questions to check comprehension	10	Effective use of the Internet
3	Creating mathematical problems for others to solve	11	Reflecting on the learning
4	Ensuring the right amount of reasoning and thinking takes place when pupils carry out investigations	12	Making links with other subjects
5	Using metacognitive principles	13	Using research
6	Encouraging individuality and innovation	14	Using quality text as a starting point for story writing
7	Using presentations	15	Expanding vocabulary
8	Working as a team	16	Tracking character/s emotions

1   Drawing on prior learning

Providing opportunities for pupils to explain what they already know so as to improve confidence levels, eg, I know that the colour of blood is red. Then to talk to a partner and compare their knowledge, etc.

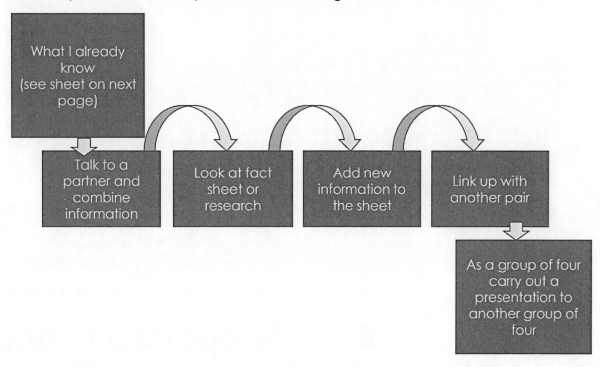

Drawing on prior learning

Linking what pupils know to new knowledge

One thing I already know about the Vikings	One thing I think I know about the Vikings	Questions I have about the Vikings

Information I now know about the Vikings	Things I am not a 100% sure about	Questions I still have about the Vikings

- Using the sheet shown top left, pupils should work on this independently in the first instance.

- They should then link with a partner and combine their knowledge.

- They should then, as a pair, be provided with a fact sheet which they should read.

- They then use the sheet to the bottom left and create a new sheet to include the combined knowledge they now have.

- They then join together with another pair. Compare their sheets, modify their sheets and work at putting together a presentation to another group of four.

Example: Science: Year 6 (1)

I know this about the way the heart works	I think I know this about the way the heart works	This is what I would like to find out about the way the heart works

Example of 'Drawing on Prior Learning' in a Year 6 context during their learning about the heart and the circulatory system

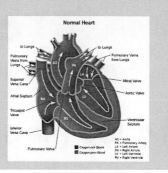

Example: Science: Year 6 (2)

- Pupils independently complete the previous sheet, outlining what they are sure about; what they are less sure about and what they would like to find out more about

- They then join a partner and share their thinking and then modify their own sheet as a result of the discussion with a partner.

- They then read the fact sheet and make amendments to their sheet as a result of the information gleaned from the fact sheet.

- The pair then join another pair and as a group of four must put together a presentation about what they know about the heart and questions they still have about the heart.

- Each group then presents their findings

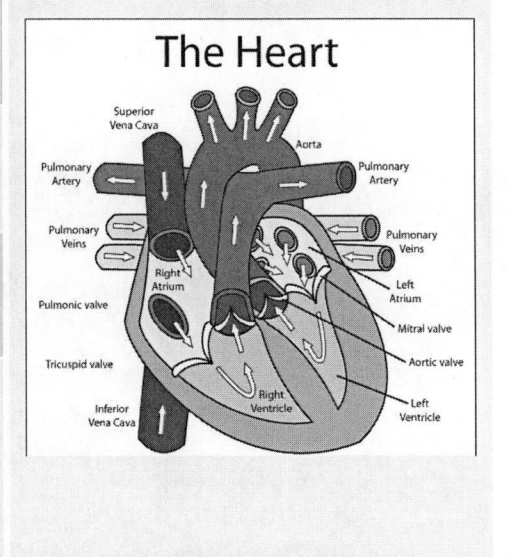

Example: Science: Year 6 (3)

Fact Sheet: How important is the heart for our well being?

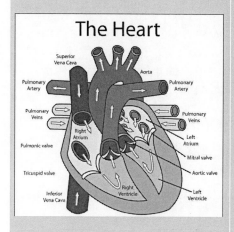

The Heart

Superior Vena Cava
Aorta
Pulmonary Artery
Pulmonary Artery
Pulmonary Veins
Pulmonary Veins
Right Atrium
Left Atrium
Pulmonic valve
Mitral valve
Tricuspid valve
Aortic valve
Inferior Vena Cava
Right Ventricle
Left Ventricle

The human **heart** is an organ that pumps blood throughout the body via the circulatory system, supplying oxygen and nutrients to the tissues and removing carbon dioxide and other wastes.

The heart's job is to collect blood from all areas of the body, pump the blood to the lungs where it receives oxygen, collect the oxygen-rich blood from the lungs, and pump it to all areas of the body.

The heart is composed of four chambers or rooms. The top two chambers are called atriums, and are the 'collecting' chambers of the heart. The bottom two chambers are called ventricles, and are the 'pumping' chambers of the heart.

The circulatory system is the body's superhighway, comprised of an intricate network of vessels that carry blood to and from all areas of your body. At the core is your heart, which pumps nutrient and oxygen-rich blood to organs so that they can function normally. Exercise and drinking lots of water are just two ways to help promote good circulation.

2 Creating questions to check comprehension

Helping pupils to understand new information

- Provide pupils with information or facts about a specific topic and let them create questions for others to answer.
- In this way they will have had to understand the text at a competent level before they can create the questions.
- I am suggesting that the amount of thinking and reasoning required is much greater if the pupils have to think of their own questions related to the text rather than answering questions about the text.
- They will need to target their questions to the right level, for example the difficulty of the questions set must be within the skill set of the pupils who are expected to answer them.

Example 1: Year 3 text on 'The role the mouth plays in breaking down food'. Pupils create three questions about the following information

How does it taste?
- When your saliva begins to break down your food, the taste buds on your tongue and on the roof of your mouth sense how the food tastes. Taste buds contain gustatory cells, which send taste signals to the brain. This is how you sense the five basic tastes of food: sour, sweet, salty, bitter, and savory. Nerves in your nose, mouth, eyes, and throat let you experience the other qualities of food, like the heat of spicy foods and the coolness of peppermint.

The role of your teeth
- Your teeth are also part of the digestive process. Teeth break down food for swallowing and further digestion. The incisors, located in the middle front of the lower and upper jaws, cut and gnaw pieces of food. The molars, in the back of the mouth, grind and chew.
- To keep your teeth at their healthiest, follow these simple preventive measures:
  - Eat a healthy diet rich in protein, fruits and vegetables, calcium, and whole grains.
  - Limit eating and drinking between meals.
  - Limit sugary foods and beverages.
  - Brush your teeth twice a day with fluoride toothpaste, and floss once a day.
  - Visit your dentist regularly for professional cleanings and exams.

Example 2: Year 3/4 text 'The Night Gardener'. Pupils create five questions about their early thoughts about what the book is about.

Questions

Look at the introduction pages and think of the title, 'The Night Gardener'.

What are your thoughts, at this time, about what the book could be about?

Think of **five** questions that you have about what the story is about at this stage.

Example 3: The Merchant and the Genius

Read the story and then think of **five** questions you have to discuss with your partner.

Think of five questions you have before discussing them with your partner.
1
2
3
4
5
Discuss your questions with your partner and then decide on three between you that you will share with the rest of the class.

Example (Sheet 1 of 2)

10 interesting facts about woodlands and forests

1	•	The main thing to know about forest and woodland habitats is that they are areas that have a lot of trees pretty close to each other.
2	•	Woodlands are a little more open than forests – woodlands have space to let a bit of light in between trees, while forests have so many trees that it's actually pretty dark when you walk around.
3	•	Trees can grow pretty much anywhere in the world, as long as it's in a spot that has enough water for them. Because of that, forest habitats can be very different depending where in the world they are.
4	•	There are many different kinds of trees, but a couple of the main groups are coniferous trees and deciduous trees.
5	•	Coniferous trees are trees that produce seeds in cones, like pine trees and spruce trees (Christmas trees!)
6	•	Deciduous trees are trees that lose their leaves in the winter, but grow them back in the summer.
7	•	Fruits and nuts found in the forest make a perfect meal for animals who live there, so they don't have to search too far to find food.
8	•	Forests also provide shelter for animals, whether it's within the tree roots or trunks, or high up in the branches.
9	•	Animals that live in forests and woodlands include big animals like bears, moose and deer, and smaller animals like hedgehogs, raccoons and rabbits
10	•	Because we use tees to make paper trees, we need to be careful about what that does to forest habitats. One way to care for forests is to recycle paper.

Example

Your Task

- Read the information set out on the previous page **'10 interesting facts about woodlands and forests'**

- You have to produce **eight questions** that will be used in a mastermind quiz.

- Your questions have to relate to the facts from the previous page.

- Your questions should have a heading:
- Your chosen subject is: **the woodlands and forests**

- Use your own ideas as much as you can. Good luck.

3   Creating mathematical problems for others to solve

To a certain extent, this is similar to the previous example except we are focusing on mathematics.

- To ensure pupils make use of their competencies in given mathematical areas. Pupils have to devise questions for their peers to solve.

- Normally, pupils confess to the fact that creating the question was far more difficult and required greater reasoning than answering the question in the first place.

- This helps to vary the tasks pupils tackle, however we need to ensure that the type of task chosen does provide the right level of challenge.

- The example on the following page is one that does provide the right balance between making use of pupils' own skills, but still requires deep thinking.

- This can be an excellent way to check on pupils' mastery.

Example 1: Mathematical problem aimed at Year 5

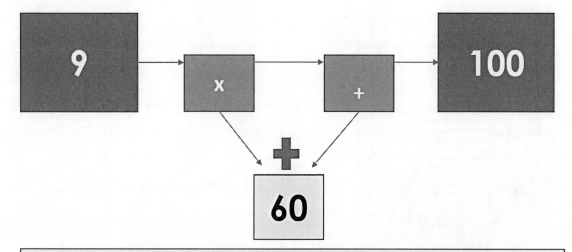

Pupils present their peers with a similar problem to the one posed above. They start by putting a number in the left hand side blue box, this number is then multiplied by a number (first orange box) and the answer is added to another number (second orange box). The answer is then placed in the right hand side blue box. The sum of the two orange boxes is then set out in the yellow box. Pupils have to find the missing numbers.

Example 2: Mathematical problem aimed at Year 4: Using negative numbers for the first time

Floor 10
Floor 9
Floor 8
Floor 7
Floor 6
Floor 5
Floor 4
Floor 3
Floor 2
Floor 1
Floor 0
Floor -1
Floor -2
Floor -3
Floor -4
Floor -5

This is a diagram of a hotel. There are 10 floors above ground and 5 floors below ground.
- The entrance is on Floor 0.
- The swimming pool is on Floor -3.
- The Laundry room is on Floor -5.
- Floor 10 is known as the penthouse.
- The restaurant is on Floor 9.

A man enters the hotel at the entrance and then goes to his room on Floor 6 before going for a swim.
How many floors will he have travelled altogether?

Now make up more examples to try out on your friends.

4 Ensuring the right amount of thinking and reasoning is taking place when carrying out investigations

Investigations in science

- When pupils are required to carry out investigations in science, too frequently the way the activity is set up sees them doing similar activities, or indeed the same activity.

- This is often because the teacher has directed the investigation too much and results in the 'reasoning and thinking' being taken away from the pupils.

- Without meaning to, the investigations ends up being a 'do it this way' activity.

- What we need is to place pupils in a position: to think for themselves; make their own mistakes; and, enjoy their own successes.

- Sometimes the over-direction can occur by providing resources that almost demand a certain way of proceeding.

- The example on the following sheet is a simple but effective way of ensuring pupils are following their own ideas.

Example: Investigation into pulse rate

Set up an investigation to find out how our pulse rate differs according to what we do.

- Initially work with a partner

- Come up with at least **four** different situations which will impact on pulse rate.

- Decide how you are going to **collect information** about pulse rate.

- Join together with another pair and share ideas

- As a group of four, come up with a way of working which will take account of your initial ideas.

- Don't forget: You will need to consider how large your sample needs to be.

- As a group of four, you will need to present your ideas and be prepared to listen to the ideas of others, being prepared to modify your own as you go forwards.

- Your main aim is to reach a conclusion as to why our pulse rates differ according to what we do.

5   Using metacognitive principles

'Considering 'Regulation'

- The following three pages focuses on helping pupils to think metacognitively by focusing on the regulation aspect of metacognition, that is, the planning, the monitoring and the evaluating.

- This would encourage pupils to maximise their thinking before they started their investigations or research by giving consideration to how well they have understood the task and making most of their critical partner.

- In addition, it encourages pupils to stop mid-way through and investigation and check that they are going down the right track. They could even 'self-question' at this stage, that is, ask questions about their own understanding.

- The evaluation stage helps pupils to reflect on the learning that has taken place and to consider how they may approach the task if they were to do it again.

- I am also suggesting that pupils are asked to write-up their investigations or research using the sub-headings: the planning stage; the monitoring or doing stage; and the evaluating stage

Example: Thinking metacognitively

Here is one example of the type of sheet that could aid better quality writing in science.

The 'Planning' stage	The 'Doing' stage	The 'Evaluative' stage
• Have I clarified exactly what the investigation/ research is about?	• Are we convinced that our ideas are the best way forwards?	• What did we get right during this investigation/ research?
• What do I consider to be the most difficult part of this research/ investigation?	• Have we seriously considered if another idea could work better?	• What would we change if we were to start again?
• What do I already know about xxxxx and jhow will this help me?	• Are we prepared to stop half way through the task and consider if we are on the right track?	• What have we learnt that we can take forward to other science/ history/ geography investigations/ researches?
• Have I been able to gather the right resources to complete the task?	• What are we learning about ourselves as learners as we carry out this investigation?	• How did this investigation/ research help us to be better scientists/ historians/ geographers?
• Is there another science/ history/ geography investigation I have done which may help me to set this one up?	• What role does my partner or other group members play in helping to clarify our thoughts?	• What could we have done to prepare ourselves better for carrying out this investigation/ research?
• Did my partner agree with the ideas I put forward?	• Have we chosen the right apparatus to carry out this investigation/ research?	• Do I find it helpful to discuss aspects of the investigation/ research with others?
• Did I take up any of my partner's ideas?		• Were our conclusions well thought through?
• How much of my original idea remains after we have created our group of four?		• What do we now know that we didn't know before we started?
		• What advice would I give others if they were to do a similar task?

Example: Suggested write-up

Title:

The Planning Stage

The Doing Stage

The Evaluating Stage

Example: Diagrams linked to the previous sheet
Graphs or diagrams to support our learning on xxxxxxx

6   Encouraging individuality and innovation

Setting out to encourage pupils to think of their own ideas when presenting information

- The main idea is to help pupils to come up with innovative ways of presenting their learning.

- In the scientific example set out in following pages, pupils are presented with just enough information and directed to a website to help them collect information.

- The role played by the critical friend is vital in helping pupils to deepen their understanding.

- Diagrams are encouraged to be used to help with the explanation.

- The aim is to provide pupils with less direction and thereby encourage as much autonomy as possible.

Year 6 Science example (1)

How does oxygen move around the body?

The heart is made of four chambers, two upper chambers and two lower chambers. Blood enters the upper chambers. These squeeze and push the blood into the lower chambers, which then squeeze and push the blood out of your heart.

1   Your heart first pumps blood to your lungs. Here, the blood picks up **oxygen** from the air that you have breathed in.

2   The blood (carrying oxygen) then travels back to your heart.

3   The heart gives the blood a second push. This time, it's sent to all the other parts of your body, including the brain, all the other organs and all the muscles. The blood delivers oxygen to them all.

4   The blood travels back to the heart, and it all begins again.

The tubes that carry blood away from your heart are called **arteries**. The tubes that carry blood back to your heart are called **veins**.

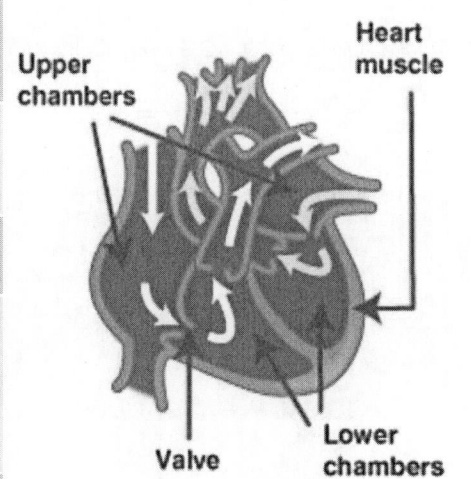

Follow:
http://www.bbc.co.uk/guides/zs8f8mn#zxchcj6
To learn more.

Year 6 Science example (2)

How does oxygen move around the body?

- Using the information from the website and reading the previous page about '**How does oxygen move around the body?**'

- Use diagrams to explain what happens.

- Set your information out in any way you want but you should link your written explanation with diagrams, where possible.

- Discuss your ideas with your critical friend before you start.

- Make sure that you have used correct scientific terminology throughout.

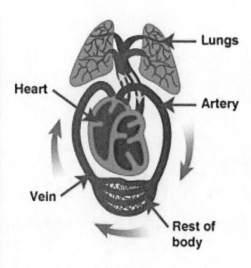

7 Using presentations

In this example, we are encouraging pupils to work in small groups and come up with different presentations

Year 4 pupils are studying the digestive system and here is a way in which experts or champions are created to focus on one specific area.

- Create six 'champion' groups and give each group one of the following features to focus on:

  - Gall bladder
  - Liver
  - Stomach
  - Mouth
  - Esophagus
  - Pancreas

- Pupils will start with the research sheet for each feature. The aim is for the group to work together to create a presentation by the end of the week. Their presentation can be as entertaining as they wish. It could contain drama, music, dance, etc.

- The following page is an example of the type of sheet provided for each champion group.

Example: Using presentations

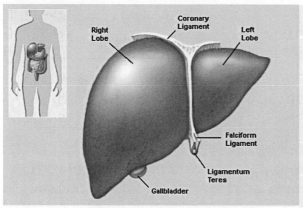

Liver

These are questions we have about the liver and what its function is.

This is what our research tells us.

Our ideas about the presentation

8 Working as a team

Create small teams, no more than four in a team

- Pupils are grouped and asked to work as a team.

- They are provided with specific task, such as researching and then each takes responsibility for one feature.

- In this case pupils know they have responsibility to others in the group.

- They may be provided with a proforma to work to as in the example set out in the following two pages.

- How much information is provided for them is dependant on age and aptitude.

- The following example is aimed at Year 3 when carrying out research about night and dark

- The idea here is that the team start together, agree who does what, work independently on their area of responsibility and come back together again to share information.

Example: Year 3 Science – Light and Dark (1)

Look at the 4 nocturnal animals below. In groups of 4, choose one each and find out 10 interesting facts about each. Then share your findings.

bats

foxes

badgers

hedgehogs

Example: Year 3 Science – Light and Dark (2)

Bats	
	Interesting Facts
1	
2	
3	
4	
5	
6	
7	
8	
9	
10	

9   Providing starting points

- **Start by providing pupils with examples**

- In this case there has to be enough variety involved in the task that follows to ensure that pupils will think of something unique to them.

- In one the example that follows, Year 3 pupils are learning about reflections and are provided with examples of photographs which show reflections.

- There is one photograph that is very different to the others so as to generate conversation and curiosity.

- Pupils are then encouraged to look for their own examples with an emphasis on uniqueness.

- They could be asked to carry on with this activity at home.

- The main aim is to create an exhibition of their photographs which has a good deal of variety.

- In the second example pupils are asked to consider shadows and are provided with examples of using their hands to create different creatures.

- Pupils are expected to work in pairs and provide their best examples which they have photographed.

Example: Providing starting points (1)

Photographic reflections

Example: Providing starting points (2)

Reflection Challenge:

Your **challenge** is to look closely at the reflection photographs on the previous page and to carefully select a subject to photograph.

You could be brave and try something unusual like the invisible girl or just aim at finding an example of reflection around the school or at home.

We are aiming to create a photographic exhibition on the theme of reflection which will be made up of all the photographs we have taken.

Example: Providing starting points (3)

Hand shadows

Here are some examples of hand shadows reflected onto a wall.
Look at these and then try and create some of your own. Your partner will ned to photograph your attempts.

Example: Providing starting points (4)

Hand shadows: My most successful ideas:

10   Effective use of the internet

Making use of the internet

- The internet has a growing number of excellent resources that can bring information to life for pupils.

- Used economically, the internet can be a brilliant source to ensure pupils are having to think more for themselves.

- Extracts can be carefully selected to help further their understanding.

- You could take one of two routes thereafter. In the first case let them use the information to describe something or let them create questions based upon what they now know.

- In the example that follows pupils have been asked to read a small extract and then watch two brief internet films.

- They are then asked to create questions for their peers to answer. They, in turn, will also receive questions from their peers.

Effective use of the internet: Science

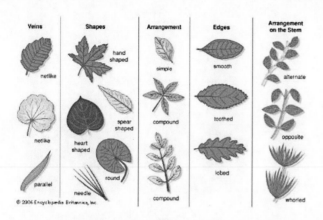

Leaves come in many different shapes. They may grow in several different arrangements.

What is the job of the leaf?

The leaf is one of the most important parts of a **plant**. Leaves produce food for the plant through a process called **photosynthesis**. The leaves of different plants vary widely in size, shape, and colour.

Use the following links to find out more about the function of the leaf.

https://www.youtube.com/watch?v=9JvioNhAwc8

https://www.youtube.com/watch?v=rUgEn6Pndgk

Effective use of the internet: Science

What is the function of leaves?

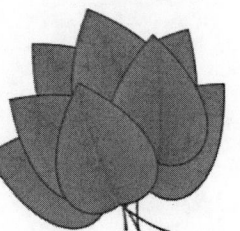
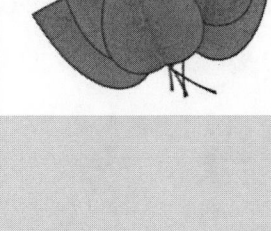

Having watched the internet extracts and read the information on the previous page, create a set of questions about the function of the leaf for others in your class to answer.

11 Reflecting on learning

Providing more opportunities for pupils to reflect on their learning

- Pupils could be asked to reflect on their learning and therefore deepen their understanding at various points.

- It is important that we build in opportunities for pupils to reflect at the end of a learning sequence. The example that follows on the next page shows one school's planning so that teachers know beforehand what is expected.

- The example that is seen two pages on shows an in-built opportunity for pupils to reflect at the end of a shorter sequence of learning, in this case their understanding about the function of the flower, stem, leaves and roots.

- In both cases the aim is to deepen understanding and to ensure pupils are provided with appropriate opportunities to evaluate their learning.

Example: Reflecting on learning (over a period of time)

Group	Learning Challenge	Focus	IT Use
Year 1	Where do the leaves go to in winter?	Pupils in groups of 4 to 5 ask the leafman questions related to the seasons. Questions then used in class book.	Morfo-booth
Year 2	Why do we love to be beside the seaside?	Re-create a scene at the seaside. Use puppet pals to bring the scenes to life.	Puppet Pals
Year 3	Who first lived in Britain?	Create a day in the life of a stone age child. Use photos and music with captions	Photo-story
Year 4	Why should the rainforests matter to us?	Groups select one of six endangered species. Make a case for the school to adopt one of the species and provide every pupil with a vote.	Power Point
Year 5	What makes the Earth angry?	Five natural disasters to be chosen: Tsunami; Earthquakes; Volcanoes; Hurricanes and Floods. Present using animoto.	Animoto
Year 6	How can we make Baildon a better place to live?	Five groups have to compete for 10 minute TV space by creating imovie selling Baildon.	imovie

Example: Reflecting on learning (within 1 week)

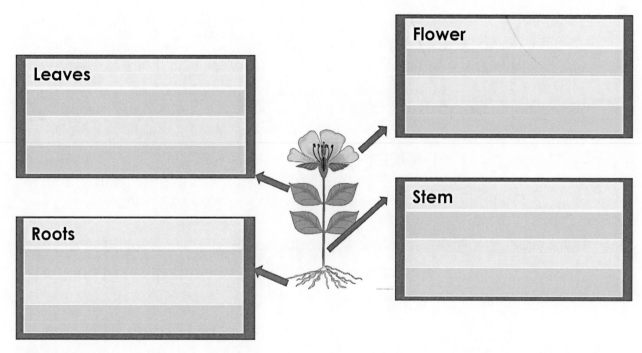

Leaves

Flower

Roots

Stem

Reflection: Using the knowledge gained from this unit use the above diagram to explain the function of: the flower; the leaves; the stem and the roots of a plant.

12   Making links with other subjects

Looking for opportunities to link different subjects

- We need to be alert to the opportunities provided for pupils to link their learning between subjects.

- Because time is so precious we need to even more aware of the opportunities to create curriculum cohesion.

- There are countless opportunities for this to happen.

- If we look at the history, geography and science subjects as our main 'drivers' we could then recognise that subjects such as: art; music; design and technology and dance provide great enhancers.

- In the example that follows the art produced by Georgia O'Keefe lends itself as an 'art enhancer' to the learning pupils are doing about the parts of a flower.

Making links with other subjects- Science & Art

Georgia O'Keefe had a unique way of capturing images of flowering plants.
Look at a range of her works.
Using the flowers provided, use pencils (HB; 4B and 8B) to make an initial sketch of the flowers you are looking at taking account of the way Georgia O'Keefe saw them.
Having completed the initial sketches use another media to create your final piece for the exhibition.
The paintings and sketches should ensure that you have captured the stamens and pistils.

13　Researching

Using research to support learning

- Encourage pupils to carry out individual research about a given topic, eg, types of spider's webs or penguins (see next 2 pages)

- Provide a focus that allows pupils to have different outcomes.

- Encourage pupils to present their outcomes in a range of different ways so as to capture unique ideas.

- The research can be focused on the internet or on a range of information books that will be available.

- Importantly, we need pupils to individually make a decision about what to include and what not to include.

Using Research: Example 1

Type of spiders' webs

- Not all spiders build the same type of web.

- Research and then create a page to show the different types of webs built by spiders.

- Draw the web and name the type of spider that builds it

- Explain why each spider builds its web in this way.

Using Research: Example 2

What can you find out about penguins?
Draw or write in the single bubble.

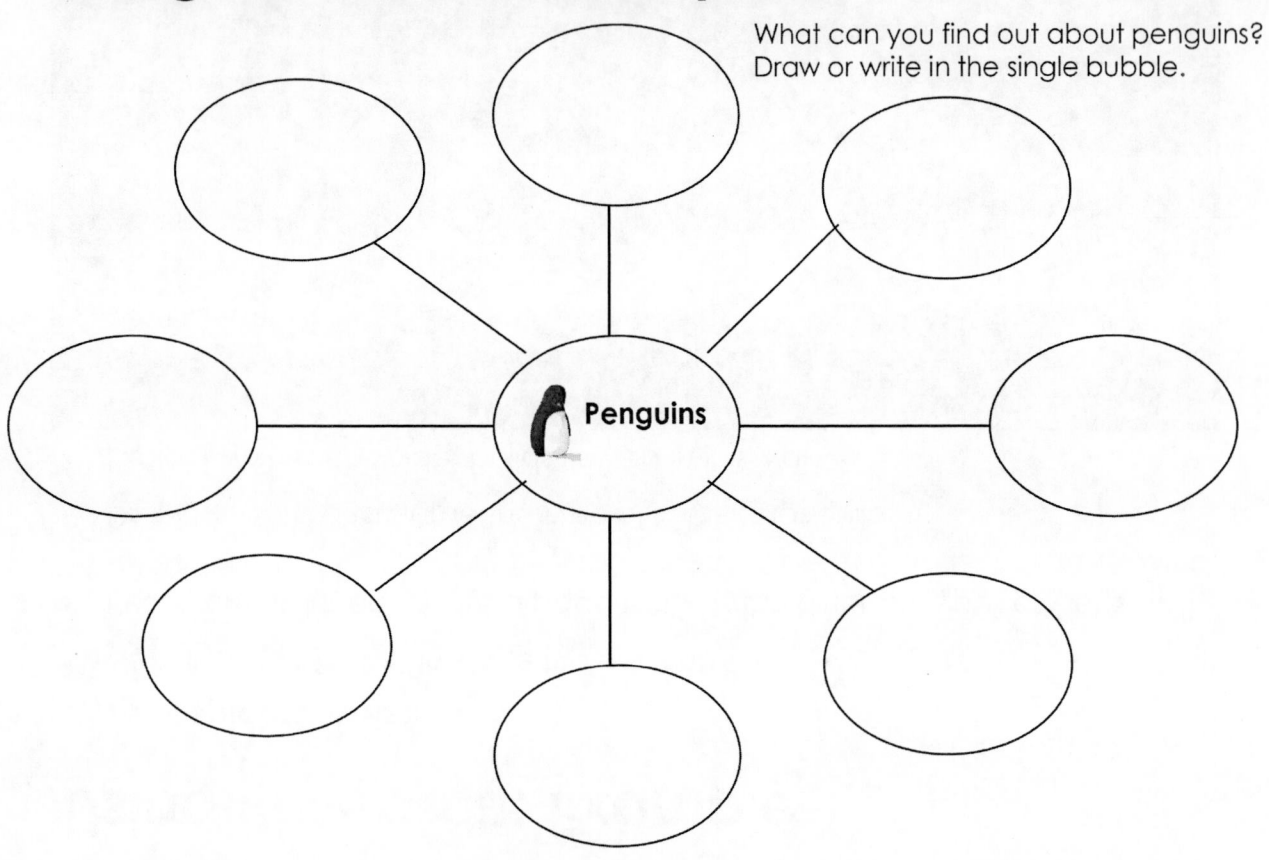

14 Using great quality literature as a starting point

Developing story writing around quality text

- Using an excellent quality text and sharing the story with pupils before focusing on one aspect.

- The following example is making use of 'Lila and the secret of rain' and focusing on the way that Lila made the sky cry to bring the much-needed rain to her village.

- In the example the pupils have to come up with a 'far-fetched' story about why do we get thunder and lightning.

- The important thing is that the pupils are absorbed in the story in the first place.

- Discuss issues arising from the original story.

- Ensure pupils make use of their critical friends to help them evaluate their stories as they are writing it.

Using quality text as a starting point: Example

After reading the book 'Lila and the secret of rain' make up a story about where thunder and lightning comes from.

You can let your imagination go wild and include as many descriptions as you can.

Possible starts:
One day the sun said to the sky..........

The beautiful blue sky saw a cloud and started to get angry with it........

15 Developing pupils' vocabulary

Enabling pupils to expand their vocabulary

- For many pupils it is the enriching of their vocabulary that is a stumbling block to attaining higher standards.

- Many schools recognise that pupils start with issues associated with their speech and language, with an impoverished vocabulary being one the issues.

- However, beyond the occasional 'word of the week' there are few proactive examples of anything being done about it.

- The following examples are ways of enabling teachers to help expand pupils' vocabulary and ensuring that pupils are using new words in everyday writing.

- The important thing is that most of these activities see pupils learning in pairs to maximise opportunities for them to say the words.

- Before pupils take on a new word as part of their vocabulary they need to say the new word at least 50 times. By learning with a partner we are providing opportunities for this to happen.

Developing vocabulary: Example 1 (Diamond 9)

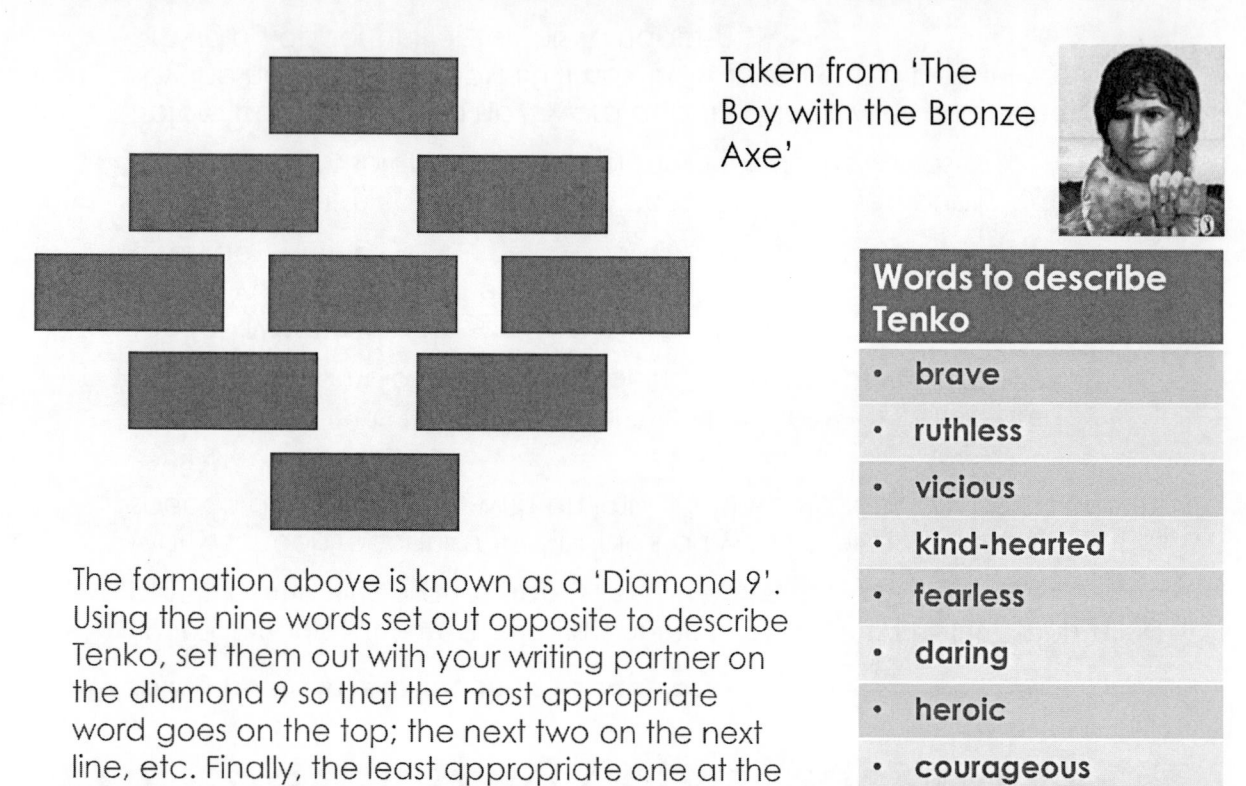

Taken from 'The Boy with the Bronze Axe'

Words to describe Tenko

- brave
- ruthless
- vicious
- kind-hearted
- fearless
- daring
- heroic
- courageous
- valiant

The formation above is known as a 'Diamond 9'. Using the nine words set out opposite to describe Tenko, set them out with your writing partner on the diamond 9 so that the most appropriate word goes on the top; the next two on the next line, etc. Finally, the least appropriate one at the bottom.

Developing vocabulary: Example 2 (Staircase)

What was Korwen's feelings towards Tenko?

Look at the list of words below:
- *jealous*
- *anger*
- *rage*
- *resentment*
- *annoyed*
- *suspicious*
- *bitter*
- *envious*

Use the staircase with a partner.
Try to agree which is the strongest word from the list and place it at the top of the stairs and then the next strongest, etc.

Korwen and Tenko

Write a set of complex sentences that captures Korwen's feelings towards Tenko.
You should aim to write eight sentences with each containing one of the words from the list

Developing vocabulary: Example 3

Challenge: Finding alternative words for nouns found in their reading

Find as many alternative words to the ones in bold below. The first one has been done for you.

boat	tribe	hut	weapon
ship			
canoe			
yacht			
ferry			
cruiser			
dinghy			
vessel			
catamaran			

Now find a noun that has significance in this story and challenge your partner to find **eight** alternative nouns

Developing vocabulary: Example 4

Starting with a target word

Target Word	**Water**		
Alternative nouns	Lake, river, stream, brook, sea, pond, spring, fountain, rain, drizzle, spray, mist, drop		1 point
Synonyms	Wet, soaked, soaking, drenched, saturated, damp, moist, water-logged		2 points
Antonyms	Dry, dusty, parched, waterless, arid		
Compound Words	Rainfall, dewdrop		
Multiple Meanings, Idioms, Proverbs etc.	Soaked to the skin Fish out of water In hot water Keep your head above water Treading water Water under the bridge Muddy the waters Still waters run deep You can lead a horse to water, but you can't make it drink Raining cats and dogs	Dry as a bone A dry run Home and dry Not a dry eye High and dry All at sea Sea level Coiled like a spring	5 Points

Start with a target word and try to collect as many points within a given time frame (suggest 5 minutes to start with)

16   Tracking character's emotions

Tracking the emotions of a character or characters as a story unfolds

- In the following two examples the story is mapped out sequentially, using pages from the book, on the horizontal axis.

- The emotional symbols are set out on the vertical axis.

- The idea is that pupils record the character's emotions at different points in the story.

- Example 1 and 2 are aimed at Key Stage 1 pupils and the key stages of the story have already been chosen.

- However, this would work equally as well for Key Stage 2 pupils but they would need to decide on the key stages from the story. In this case the horizontal axis would be empty.

- Example 3 could be used with older pupils who would decide on the key stages of the myth themselves.

Tracking Emotions: Example 1: Wild by Emily Hughes

How does the girl feel during the story?

R

Tracking Emotions: Example 2: Beegu by Alexis Deacon

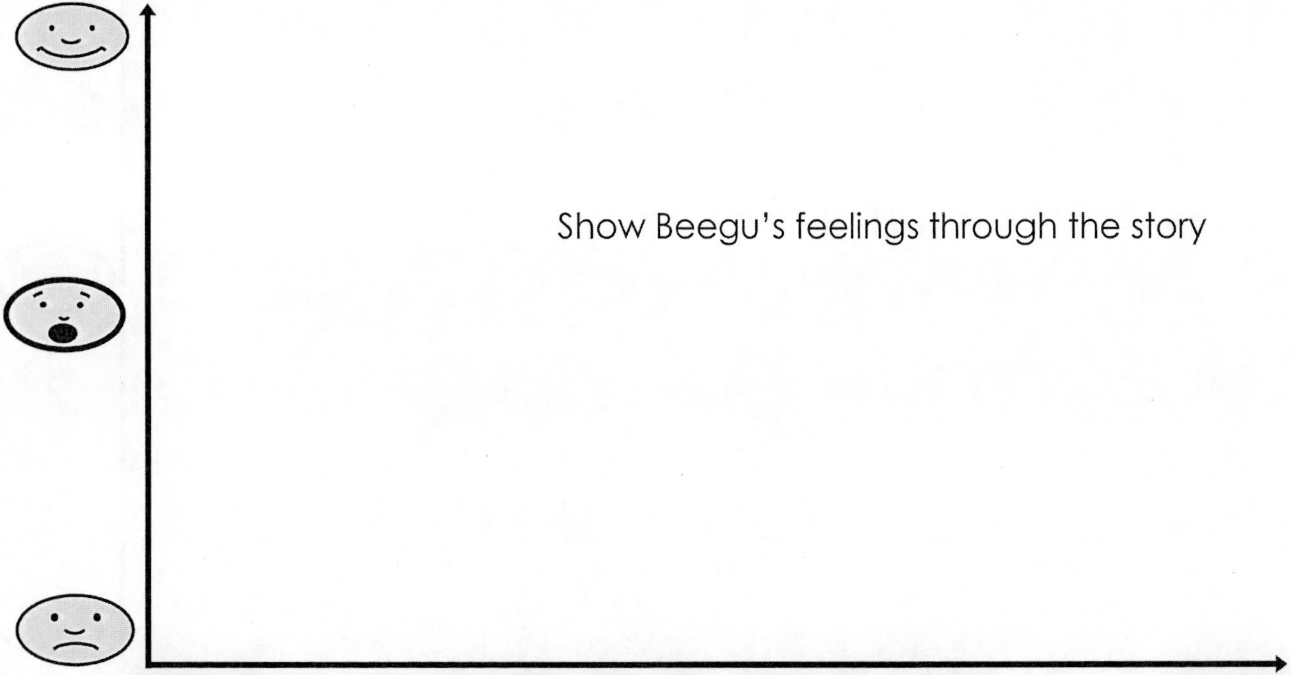

Show Beegu's feelings through the story

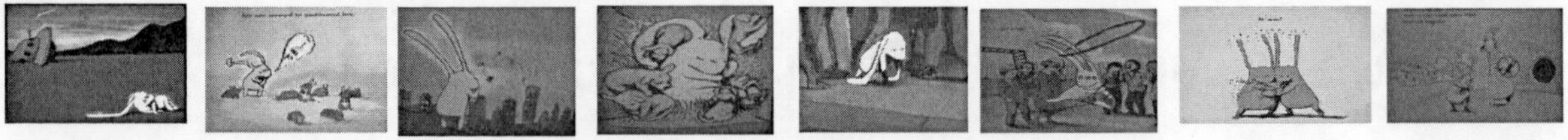

Tracking Emotions: Example 3:
Greek Myths by Marcia Williams

How do Theseus' feelings change during the story?